To:

From:

Owl
Wisdom

Compiled by Vicki Fischer
and Suzanne Schwalb

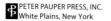
PETER PAUPER PRESS, INC.
White Plains, New York

For David and Robert

Designed by Margaret Rubiano

Copyright © 2014
Peter Pauper Press, Inc.
202 Mamaroneck Avenue
White Plains, NY 10601
All rights reserved
ISBN 978-1-4413-1592-2
Printed in China
7 6 5 4 3 2 1

Owl
Wisdom

Be happy. It's one way of being wise.

Colette

Long associated with wisdom, prophecy, even strength and wealth, owls feature in this compendium of inspiration. (You've chosen wisely, fledgling reader!) Take wing with the endearing characters depicted here and get a bird's-eye view of

life, the world, and owls themselves. And let a host of philosophers, writers, wits, and wags offer you words of wisdom, too. Swoop in for some sagacity and mystical musings— our jolly owls will cheer you on.

The heart is wiser than the intellect.

J. G. Holland

The love of
wisdom begins
in wonder.

Socrates

Wisdom comes from experience. Experience is often a result of lack of wisdom.

Terry Pratchett

Fly without
wings,
Dream with
open eyes,
See in
darkness.

Dejan Stojanovic

The more
boundless your
vision, the more
real you are.

Deepak Chopra

Good people
are good because
they've come to
wisdom through
failure.

William Saroyan

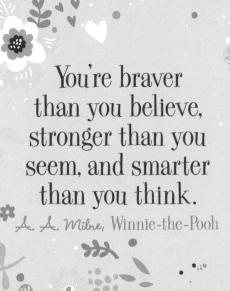

You're braver
than you believe,
stronger than you
seem, and smarter
than you think.

A. A. Milne, Winnie-the-Pooh

He who
begins is half
done. Dare to
be wise. Make
a beginning.

Horace

Sometimes
you can't
see yourself
clearly
until you
see yourself
through
the eyes
of others.

Ellen DeGeneres

True wisdom
lies in
gathering
the precious
things out of
each day as
it goes by.

E. S. Bouton

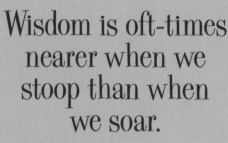

Wisdom is oft-times nearer when we stoop than when we soar.

William Wordsworth

I'm youth, I'm joy,
I'm a little bird
that has broken
out of the egg.

J. M. Barrie, Peter Pan

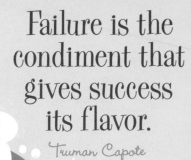

Failure is the
condiment that
gives success
its flavor.

Truman Capote

Hold on firmly
to good friends
and fine
teachers. Riches
and power are
fleeting dreams,
but the fragrance
of wise words
lingers in
the world.

Hanshan

It's the simple
things in life that
are the most
extraordinary; only
wise men are able to
understand them.

Paulo Coelho, The Alchemist

It is not only fine feathers that make fine birds.

Aesop

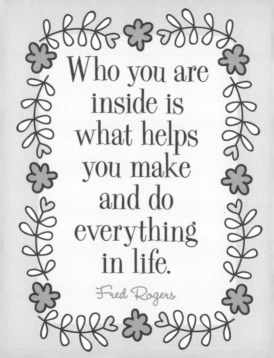

Who you are inside is what helps you make and do everything in life.

Fred Rogers

A word to the wise
ain't necessary—it's
the stupid ones that
need the advice.

Bill Cosby

But ah! If we could
perceive the world of
the owl, what strange
sounds and beautiful
forms we might enjoy!

Robert W. Nero

Even when you have doubts, take that step. Take chances. Mistakes are never a failure—they can be turned into wisdom.

Cat Cora

The supreme human good is wisdom.

St. Augustine

I rejoice
that there
are owls.

Henry David Thoreau,
Walden

Life can only be understood backwards, but it must be lived forwards.

Sören Kierkegaard

No brain is
stronger than
its weakest
think.

Thomas L. Masson

Wisdom
leads us back
to childhood.

Blaise Pascal

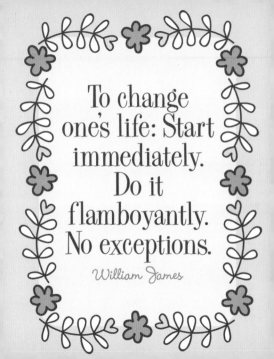

To change
one's life: Start
immediately.
Do it
flamboyantly.
No exceptions.

William James

If I had to
live my life again,
I'd make the same
mistakes, only
sooner.

Tallulah Bankhead

Turn your wounds into wisdom.

Oprah Winfrey

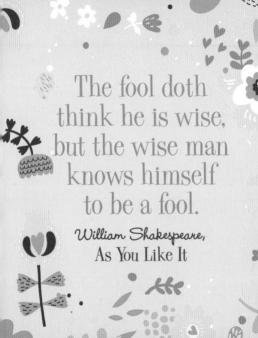

The fool doth
think he is wise,
but the wise man
knows himself
to be a fool.

William Shakespeare,
As You Like It

Nothing can
be wiser than
fairy wisdom.
It is as true
as sunbeams.

Douglas Jerrold

I hoot to waken
those that sleep,
As soon as day's first
beams do peep;
That they may rise,
and say their prayers,
And not be caught in
this world's cares.

W. H. D. Rouse's
King Solomon and the Owl

You can tell whether a man is clever by his answers. You can tell whether a man is wise by his questions.

Naguib Mahfouz

Hope is the thing
with feathers
That perches in the soul
And sings the tune
without the words
And never stops at all.

Emily Dickinson

The clearest
way into the
Universe is
through a forest
wilderness.

John Muir

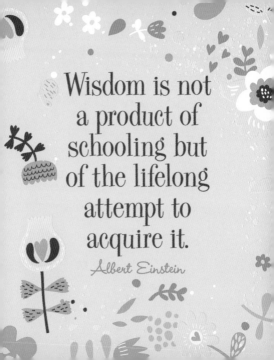

Wisdom is not a product of schooling but of the lifelong attempt to acquire it.

Albert Einstein

If you soar
with the eagles
during the day,
you can't hoot
with the owls
at night.

Sometimes
life is owl
a matter of
perspective.

The art of
being wise
is the art
of knowing
what to
overlook.

William James

Common sense in an uncommon degree is what the world calls wisdom.

Samuel Taylor Coleridge

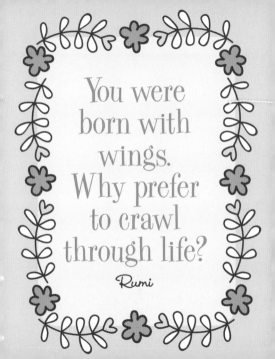

People often claim
to hunger for truth,
but seldom like
the taste when it's
served up.

George R. R. Martin,
A Clash of Kings

Only a fool learns
from his own
mistakes. The wise
man learns from the
mistakes of others.

Otto von Bismarck

The well-bred
contradict
other people. The
wise contradict
themselves.

Oscar Wilde

It takes
two wings
to fly.

Eric Schaub

Our task must
be to free ourselves
... by widening our
circle of compassion
to embrace all
living creatures and
the whole of nature
and its beauty.

Albert Einstein

Wisdom doesn't
come only from
the experience
you have had,
but from the
experience you
have chosen
not to have.

Anthony Marais

It is the province
of knowledge to speak
and it is the privilege
of wisdom to listen.

Oliver Wendell Holmes

Never, never rest
contented with
any circle of
ideas, but always
be certain that
a wider one is
still possible.

Richard Jefferies

The owl is the
wisest of all birds
because the more
it sees, the less it
talks.

African proverb

You can't stay in your corner of the Forest waiting for others to come to you. You have to go to them sometimes.

A. A. Milne,
Winnie-the-Pooh

The next best thing
to being wise oneself

is to live in a circle
of those who are.

C. S. Lewis

What you are
is what you
have been.
What you'll
be is what
you do now.

Buddha

Patience is the key to
success. Wisdom is
knowing that success
doesn't happen overnight.

Proverb

Never assume
the obvious
truth is true.

William Safire

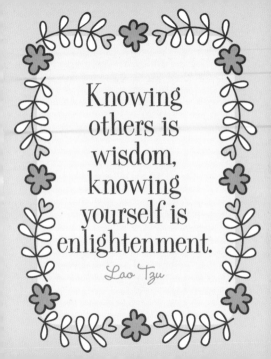

Knowing
others is
wisdom,
knowing
yourself is
enlightenment.

Lao Tzu

We
need the
tonic of
wildness.

Henry David Thoreau,
Walden

Let your vision
be world-embracing,
rather than
confined to your
own self.

Bahá'u'lláh

Peace
Love
Owls